Written by
Mary Lyn Ray

Illustrated by
Giselle Potter

Once Upon a Fairy Tale House

The True Story of Four Sisters and the Magic They Built

Beach Lane Books
New York   London   Toronto   Sydney   New Delhi

Santa Barbara, 1902

On long summer afternoons, four sisters on Victoria Street were often in the shade of a garden, reading their favorite fairy tales.

Mildred and Harriett and Brenda and Wilma wished they could live in those stories. But they hadn't found a way in.

Still, summer wasn't only books, especially when the ocean was so near they could walk there.

Mildred liked to draw
what she saw at the beach.

Harriett liked to build
castles from what the
tides brought up.

Brenda liked to count things she found there.

And Wilma liked to make and unmake hills and mountains with a toy steam shovel someone had left behind.

When the sun began to drop toward dusk, they met
their parents for proper tea with china cups at the
beach pavilion. Or they had a picnic on a blanket
spread across the sand.

Wisps of talk floated around them, like smoke from
the scattered fires where some people gathered
driftwood and lingered long past dark.

But Mildred and Harriett and Brenda and Wilma
were mostly listening to something else. As waves
rolled in and the tide slid back toward the sea,
at its edge they heard the whisper of stories, the way
stories are just before they have words.

This was their secret, kept for bedtime,
when they invented their own fairy tales.

They wished they could live in those, too.
But it was starting to look as if they would
have to wish harder—

until one night Wilma said, "We could
imagine fairy tale *houses* and pretend
we live in them."

So each drew her own house
in her head.

And there, in their dreams,
they slept every night.

When morning came, Mildred and Harriett and Brenda and Wilma never sat around, wondering what to do. One or another always had an idea that was improved by including all four.

They played and explored and wondered and wished.

And summer by summer (and in between) they also grew up.

Mildred became an artist hired by a furniture store to decorate tables and chairs and beds and armoires. All day she stood in the store window, painting. And people on the sidewalk stood at the glass, watching. Mildred's job made her happy.

Until styles changed.

When customers wanted a new, modern look to go with new, modern houses, the fun and curls were gone from her work.

So Mildred left the city and came home—where her sisters understood, the way sisters do. "You must have a place," said Brenda, "where you can paint what you want to paint."

Harriett began sketching a studio. And when the others saw it, they clapped: it looked like a fairy tale house.

All they needed was a builder.

But each they went to said, "No one can build that."

Making plans for houses and making houses from drawings was, however, Harriett's everyday work. Because she had become an architect.

So she drew plans to match the sketch, pulled on overalls, and said, "I guess I'll have to show them."

And that was how it came about, just where
land turned to sea and tides whispered,
that a studio began to grow.

Mildred could return to her brushes.

People could again watch her paint. And there they
fell under the spell of the fairy tale house: its odd little
windows and storybook doors, the walls that weren't
straight, and the roof like a mother hen's wings.

Then some people realized they didn't want a modern house. They wanted a fairy tale one. And Mildred and Harriett knew how that could happen.

Harriett would draw plans and oversee the construction. Mildred would decorate the inside the way she decorated furniture.

There was only one problem. Who would order the lumber and bricks and shingles and nails? Who would keep account of what was paid and what was due?

The builders couldn't if they were building.

Harriett couldn't if she was designing the houses and supervising the builders.

Mildred couldn't if she was painting shelves and stairs and cupboards and doors.

But they had a sister who had always liked to count things. And she had become a banker. So they went to Brenda. And Brenda agreed to take care of business.

They were set to begin, until they remembered: before you can build a house, you have to prepare a place to put it. You need someone who can drive a shovel and dozer.

Brenda couldn't if she was ordering lumber and adding up numbers.

Harriett couldn't if she was in charge of the builders and drawing plans for more houses.

Mildred couldn't if she was painting decorations.

And none of them knew, anyway, how to work a steam shovel. But they had a sister who used to.

Except Wilma had also gone into banking and business. She couldn't dig foundations. She could, however, help Brenda keep accounts and sell houses.

So they hired someone else
to run the shovel and dozer
as people stood by, watching.

More came to watch the cottages bloom.

And when everything was ready, movers carried tables and beds and chairs and boxes into each house.

Then families arrived.

And one by one they noticed . . .

something seemed to hover there—

especially when the scent of gardens spread
across a day, or nights were still enough to hear
the ocean, or sea fog made the familiar strange.

No one ever said exactly what they saw
in dappled shade or moon shadows . . .
or what explained some things that happened.

But Mildred and Harriett and Brenda
and Wilma were pretty sure.

Because they knew about fairy tale magic.

Author's Note

Mildred, Harriett, Brenda, and Wilma Moody were born in Santa Barbara, California, just as the nineteenth century was ending. It was there and in nearby Montecito that they grew up and lived their lives. In the summer of 1902, Mildred was almost six, Harriett had just turned eleven, Brenda was nine, and Wilma was almost four. They also had a brother, Bert, who was thirteen. But, as sisters, they were accustomed to approaching the world as a confederation of four.

At the time, it was not common for women to be artists or architects or engineers or bankers or business professionals: those choices were usually reserved for men. Mildred and Harriett and Brenda and Wilma showed a different narrative was possible. Yet even as they embraced their adult lives, they also demonstrated that growing up didn't require surrendering the wonder they'd known up close in childhood.

After Mildred earned a degree in art, she began teaching high school classes, but she missed being able to do her own painting. So she went to Barker Brothers Furniture in Los Angeles, which she called "a long hundred miles from home." There she worked from 1922 to 1930 and became assistant manager of the art department. Her specialty was rosemaling, an old European style of painted floral decoration. But when customers started wanting an undecorated, modern look, rosemaling became outdated.

In the meantime, after studying architecture, engineering, and technical drawing, Harriett had been appointed assistant city engineer for Santa Barbara. Wilma worked in banking, and Brenda was both a banker and a realtor, as well as the county recorder of deeds. With a sure eye for prime real estate, she had bought a lot on the Old Coast Highway (now Coast Village Road) in Montecito. So when Mildred came home and needed a studio, the sisters knew just where to build it.

I first read about the Moody sisters, and what they called their pixie cottages, in 1989 in an issue of *Victoria* magazine given to me by a friend. I was only beginning to write picture books and was intrigued by the story the sisters had lived. Wanting to see these houses and meet Mildred, then ninety-three, I wrote to her to ask if I could come visit. She promptly wrote back, "Yes, do!" So that September I set out from New Hampshire. My own sister came with me on the long journey, four days by train from Boston to Chicago to Montecito. Anticipating our arrival and wondering how she would know us, Mildred sent two paper corsages (one a pink rose and the other a rose the color of a beach sunset) cut from a seed catalogue. Pinning them on as our train arrived, we entered her world.

Mildred's house on Pimiento Lane was a museum of grand paintings, antiques, and souvenirs from distant travel. Books and projects were everywhere. Outside were California gardens. And inside and out, there were ceramic pixies like the ones she had left in each cottage (on a mantel, in a cupboard, or somewhere) to protect, Mildred said, each home and those who came to it.

Visiting the cottages with Mildred, I saw that she and her sisters hadn't been only building houses. They were making places that story could come to, where *Once upon a time* could continue—and did. These weren't, however, attempts to reproduce fairy tale houses exactly. They were a mix of ideas remembered from picture books and Old English half-timbering and thatch, married to sensible, contemporary design— and other enchantment.

In the 1930s, with America in the grip of the Great Depression, some owners of grand manor houses nearby couldn't afford to keep them or pay taxes on them, and other people couldn't afford to buy them. So they were being torn down, and the house parts and furnishings were sold at estate sales. Mildred and Harriett bought carved paneling, doors, beams, cupboards, mantels, and diamond-paned windows that already held a memory of *Long ago and far away*. They incorporated these into their cottages, adding bookcases, window seats, and nooks and crannies because they understood there must be places for reading and wishing and wondering and dreaming.

Beginning with the studio for Mildred in 1930, the sisters created some thirty houses, now known as Moody cottages. D. H. MacQuiddy, the local contractor who agreed to build the studio when no one else would, went on to build all of the cottages.

At the estate sales, the sisters also bought antique furniture they intended to use in the cottages. But the houses, Mildred said, "were often too small for the furniture." So they began selling antiques at her studio, which had a tearoom, too. Their location on the Old Coast Highway, as Brenda had anticipated, brought traffic and attention, and their enterprise flourished. After some years they closed the tearoom (because "it was too much work," said Mildred), but they continued offering antiques, combined with interior decorating, until the 1960s.

The Moody sisters never lived in one of their cottages. They needed more room for all four of them. So in 1937 they bought a redwood-shingled, converted farmhouse, which was then out in the country, in Montecito. Called The Peppers, it had been enlarged by architect Julia Morgan and restyled by the celebrated decorator Elsie de Wolfe. There the sisters lived happily and expansively for thirty years, observing, said Mildred, "the magic that life could bring." They were known for their hospitality and for relishing the arts. Then time and age brought changes. After Brenda died in 1965, and Harriett in 1966, Mildred and Wilma sold The Peppers in 1969 and moved to Pimiento Lane. Wilma died in 1981 and Mildred in 1996, only months short of one hundred.

The Moody sisters—and their cottages—had, however, already become legend. And in that place where waves still roll in, whispering stories, the magic they sheltered continues.

For Mildred and her sisters,
and for my own
—M. L. R.

For the magical sisters,
Pia and Izzy
—G. P.

BEACH LANE BOOKS • An imprint of Simon & Schuster Children's Publishing Division • 1230 Avenue of the Americas, New York, New York 10020 • Text © 2023 by Mary Lyn Ray • Illustration © 2023 by Giselle Potter • Book design by Lauren Rille © 2023 by Simon & Schuster, Inc. • All rights reserved, including the right of reproduction in whole or in part in any form. • BEACH LANE BOOKS and colophon are trademarks of Simon & Schuster, Inc. • For information about special discounts for bulk purchases, please contact Simon & Schuster Special Sales at 1-866-506-1949 or business@simonandschuster.com. • The Simon & Schuster Speakers Bureau can bring authors to your live event. For more information or to book an event, contact the Simon & Schuster Speakers Bureau at 1-866-248-3049 or visit our website at www.simonspeakers.com. • The text for this book was set in Belizio. • The illustrations for this book were rendered in ink and watercolor on paper. • Manufactured in China • 0123 SCP
First Edition
10 9 8 7 6 5 4 3 2 1
Library of Congress Cataloging-in-Publication Data
Names: Ray, Mary Lyn, author. | Potter, Giselle, illustrator. • Title: Once upon a fairy tale house: the true story of four sisters and the magic they built / Mary Lyn Ray ; illustrated by Giselle Potter. • Description: First edition. | New York : Beach Lane Books, [2023] | Includes bibliographical references. | Audience: Ages 0–8 | Audience: Grades 2–3 | Summary: "A picture book biography of the four Moody sisters who designed and built fairy tale-like cottages in Santa Barbara in the 1930s and 1940s"—Provided by publisher. • Identifiers: LCCN 2021056476 (print) | LCCN 2021056477 (ebook) | ISBN 9781481479820 (hardcover) | ISBN 9781481479837 (ebook) • Subjects: LCSH: Moody family—Juvenile literature. | Sisters—California—Santa Barbara—Biography—Juvenile literature. | Cottages—California—Santa Barbara—Juvenile literature. | Fantastic architecture—California—Santa Barbara—Juvenile literature. | Santa Barbara (Calif.)—Biography—Juvenile literature. | Classification: LCC F869.S45 R39 2023 (print) | LCC F869.S45 (ebook) | DDC 979.4/91—dc23/eng/20220309 • LC record available at https://lccn.loc.gov/2021056476 • LC ebook record available at https://lccn.loc.gov/2021056477